Table of Contents

What things do potato plants need to grow?

One Row at a Time

Potatoes grow under the ground. A potato harvester gathers potatoes.

A tractor pulls the harvester.
The harvester moves through
one row at a time.

Blades and Chains

A **blade** cuts into the soil. It goes under the potatoes.

The potatoes are lifted onto the **primary chain**. Soil and rocks come up, too.

What do potatoes feel
like to touch?

The potatoes travel over more chains. The soil falls through the chains.

Into the Truck

The potatoes go to a platform. Workers take out rocks and **vines**.

A truck moves next to the harvester. A **conveyor** carries the potatoes to the truck.

Lots of Food!

The truck is full of potatoes!

What do potatoes taste like?

Potatoes are an important food. People eat them all over the world.

Find Out More

Weiss, Ellen. *From Eye to Potato*. Danbury, CT: Children's Press, 2007.

United States Potato Board—Potato Goodness: Kids Corner
www.potatogoodness.com/my-potatoes/home-cooks/kids-corner/
Find recipes, coloring pages, and activities all about potatoes.

Glossary

blade (BLAYD) the cutting part of a tool

conveyor (kuhn-VAY-ur) a device for carrying things from place to place

primary chain (PRYE-mair-ee CHAYN) the first chain on a potato harvester

vines (VINEZ) the long, creeping stems of potato plants and other plants

Home and School Connection

Use this list of words from the book to help your child become a better reader. Word games and writing activities can help beginning readers reinforce literacy skills.

a	eat	lifted	potato	too
all	falls	like	potatoes	touch
and	feel	lots	primary	tractor
are	food	moves	pulls	travel
at	full	need	rocks	truck
blade	gathers	next	row	under
blades	go	of	soil	up
carries	goes	one	take	vines
chain	ground	onto	taste	what
chains	grow	out	the	workers
come	harvester	over	things	world
conveyor	important	people	through	
cuts	into	plants	time	
do	it	platform	to	

Index

About the Author

Samantha Bell is a children's book writer, illustrator, teacher, and mom of four busy kids. Her articles, short stories, and poems have been published online and in print.